I WONDER

HOW CARS ARE MADE

Neil Curtis and Peter Greenland

HEINEMANN

Many people travel by car each day.
Cars carry people quickly
from one place to another.
Some roads have lots of cars on them.

Cars are made of
steel, plastic, rubber, and cloth.
Some parts of a car are made of
aluminium, copper, or glass.

Before a new car is made, the designer first sketches on paper several ideas.
The sketches show what the new car will look like.

The car makers choose the best sketch and make a full-sized model of the new car. This model is measured very carefully.

An engineer then makes
a plan of the engine and decides
how the other moving parts
in the car will work.
The engineer feeds all these details into
a computer which draws a model
of the whole car on the screen.

Giant pressing machines are used to
press out and cut sheets of steel.
The sheets of steel will make the car's
body panels and frames.

The panels and frames are
held in place by another machine.
A team of robots joins the pieces of
the metal together by welding them.
Welding uses heat to soften the metal
before the pieces are hammered together.

A computer uses cameras and
beams of light to look at
the finished body.
The computer checks that all the parts
are in the correct place.

The steel body is cleaned thoroughly.
It is bright and shiny.
Then it is coated with chemicals to
stop it going rusty.

All of the body's joints are
sealed with a plastic coat.
Then the [illegible] painted with
sever[illegible]al paint.

Many new car bodies are lined up.
They move along a conveyor
for each part of the car
to be added in turn.

The wires for the car's electricity
are put in the body and
the lights are added.
Padding is put into parts of the car
to deaden the noise of the engine.

More robots help to fix
all of the car's windows and screens.

The engine has been made
in another part of the factory.
The engine is now lifted into the car.
Then the steering and brakes go in.

The wheels are fitted to the car.
The engine must be connected
to the wheels.
The connection is called transmission.

Carpets are laid inside the car.
Linings are put into the front and sides of the car.
These linings inside the car are called the trim.

The seats are put inside the car.
They are covered with plastic to
keep them clean.

At last, the doors are fitted to the car.
A robot holds the door in place while
a fitter bolts it on firmly.
Another fitter completes the work.

Water is put in the car's radiator
to keep the engine cool when it is going.
Oil helps to make
the engine run smoothly.
The petrol tank is filled with fuel.

The car is tested very carefully before
it is sent to the car showroom.
Every part of it must work properly.
The car is covered with wax to protect it
from dirt, sunshine, and rain.

Cars are loaded on to a big truck called
a car transporter which
takes them to the garages where
they will be sold.

The finished car goes to the showroom.
Then it is cleaned and polished.
At last, it is sold to its proud owner.

Index

The author wishes to thank Alan Joiner of Rover Group Limited for his assistance and co-operation during the preparation of this book.

HEINEMANN CHILDREN'S REFERENCE
a division of Heinemann Educational Books Ltd
Halley Court, Jordan Hill, Oxford OX2 8EJ

OXFORD LONDON EDINBURGH
MELBOURNE SYDNEY AUCKLAND
MADRID ATHENS BOLOGNA
SINGAPORE IBADAN NAIROBI HARARE
GABORONE KINGSTON PORTSMOUTH NH(USA)

ISBN 0 431 00256 8

For Cataloguing in Publication Data please apply to the British Library

First published 1990

Editorial consultant: Donna Bailey
Designed and produced by Curtis Garratt Limited
The Old Vicarage, Horton cum Studley, Oxford OX9 1BT

All photographs by Peter Greenland except:
4, 5, 6, 7, 8, 9, 10, 11, 14, 15 by kind permission of Rover Group Limited

Printed in Hong Kong

90 91 92 93 94 95 10 9 8 7 6 5 4 3 2 1